MACMILLAN READERS

BEGINNER LEVEL

LOUISA M. ALCOTT

Good Wives

Retold by Anne Collins

Founding Editor: John Milne

The Macmillan Readers provide a choice of enjoyable reading materials for learners of English. The series is published at six levels – Starter, Beginner, Elementary, Pre-intermediate, Intermediate and Upper.

Level control
Information, structure and vocabulary are controlled to suit the students' ability at each level.

The number of words at each level:

Starter	about 300 basic words
Beginner	about 600 basic words
Elementary	about 1100 basic words
Pre-intermediate	about 1400 basic words
Intermediate	about 1600 basic words
Upper	about 2200 basic words

Vocabulary
Some difficult words and phrases in this book are important for understanding the story. Some of these words are explained in the story and some are shown in the pictures. From Pre-intermediate level upwards, words are marked with a number like this: ...[3]. These words are explained in the Glossary at the end of the book.

Contents

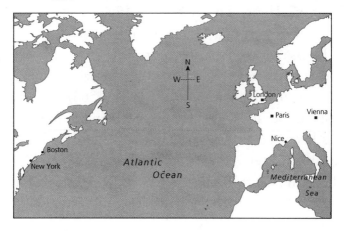

A Note About the Author

Louisa May Alcott was American. She was born on 29th November 1832. She lived in the town of Concord, Massachusetts, in the east of North America. Louisa's father was Amos Bronson Alcott. He was a teacher and a philosopher. Louisa had three sisters – May, Elizabeth and Anna.

Louisa did not go to school. She learnt her lessons in her home. She was intelligent. She liked books. Louisa read all the books in her father's library. She also talked with her father's friends, Ralph Waldo Emerson, Henry Thoreau and Nathaniel Hawthorne. These men were famous writers and poets.

Louisa wrote her first story in 1863. She wrote poems and stories for books and magazines. Louisa's most popular book was *Little Women* (1868). The book is about four girls – Amy, Meg, Beth and Jo March. In this book, Louisa was writing about her own life and about her sisters. Amy March is May Alcott and Meg is Elizabeth Alcott. Beth March is Anna Alcott and Jo is Louisa herself. In 1869, Louisa wrote a second part to this story – *Good Wives*.

Some of her other stories are: *An Old-fashioned Girl* (1870), *Little Men* (1871), *Eight Cousins* (1875), *Rose in Bloom* (1876) and *Jo's Boys* (1886).

Louisa Alcott never married. She visited Europe in 1871. After her return to America, she lived in Boston. She worked for women's rights. She often wrote about the lives of independent women. Louisa May Alcott died in Boston on 6th March 1888.

A Note About This Story

Time: 1866 to 1877. **Places:** The United States of America and Europe.

———

Several of the people in this story travel from America to Europe by ship. Before 1838, this journey was very difficult. People had to travel in sailing ships. Sometimes there were no winds in the Atlantic Ocean. Then the journey was very long. But in 1838, a steamship crossed the Atlantic Ocean for the first time. In 1840, Samuel Cunard – a Canadian ship-owner – started Atlantic crossings between America and Britain. Cunard had four big steamships. Every week, a ship sailed from America to England, and another ship sailed from England to America. This was a journey of fourteen days. By the 1860s, the ships' engines were better, and the journey was faster. It became a popular journey. Many rich Americans crossed the Atlantic Ocean and visited Europe.

The People in This Story

Mr March
ˈmɪstə mɑːtʃ

Mrs March ('Marmee')
ˈmɪsɪz mɑːtʃ

Aunt March
ɑːnt mɑːtʃ

Meg March
meg mɑːtʃ

John Brooke
dʒɒn brʊk

Jo March
dʒəʊ mɑːtʃ

Beth March
beθ mɑːtʃ

Amy March
ˈeɪmi mɑːtʃ

Laurie Laurence
ˈlɒri ˈlɒrəns

Mr Laurence
ˈmɪstə ˈlɒrəns

Professor Bhaer
prəˈfesər beər

Mrs Carrol
ˈmɪsɪz ˈkærəl

6

1

Meg's Wedding

This book is a story about four sisters – Meg, Jo, Beth and Amy March. They lived in a small town in the state of Massachusetts, in North America.

Mr March, the girls' father, was a minister. He worked at a church in the town. Five years before the beginning of this story, the American Civil war had started. Mr March had left his home, and for two years he had worked at a hospital for soldiers. During this time, Mrs March took care of the four girls alone. Mr March had worked hard at the hospital and he had become ill. In December 1863, he returned home. For the next three years, the March family lived together quietly and happily.

In December 1866, Meg March was twenty years old, Jo was nineteen, Beth was seventeen and Amy was sixteen. For three years, Meg had been engaged to marry a clever young man – John Brooke. Meg and John wanted to get married the next summer.

John Brooke had been Laurie Laurence's teacher. Laurie was the Marches' neighbour and he was Jo March's special friend. Laurie's parents were dead. For most of his life, he had lived with his grandfather in the big house next to the Marches' little house. But in 1864, Laurie Laurence had left the little town. After that, he lived at his college in Boston. John Brooke's work in the Laurence house had finished and John joined the army. He fought in the war for a year, then he returned to the small town. He was injured, but he soon became well again. He got a job in an office in the town. He wanted to be near Meg.

John Brooke was a good, kind man, but he was not rich. He did not earn much money. At the beginning of 1867, he bought a small house near the Marches' house. Meg loved this little house and she had many plans for it.

Meg's sisters made many pretty, useful things for the house. All that spring, they worked hard. At last, in June, the house was ready.

'Are you happy with the house, Meg?' asked Mrs March one day. 'Soon, it will be your home.'

Meg smiled at her mother. The sisters had always called Mrs March 'Marmee'. They still called her that.

'Yes, Marmee,' said Meg. 'I'm very happy. I love our little house. And in one week, I will be John's wife.'

'You must have a servant, Meg,' said Amy, the youngest sister. 'Someone must cook and clean for you.'

'Oh, no. I don't want a servant,' said Meg. 'I will take care of everything myself. I'll be very happy to do that.'

———

Meg and John got married at the end of June. Meg made her own wedding dress. She and John invited only a few people to the wedding – their families and some good friends. Laurie Laurence came home from college for the wedding. His grandfather was at the wedding too, and so was Aunt March. Aunt March was a very old lady. She was Mr March's older sister.

The day of the wedding was a beautiful summer day. Meg put on her dress. Her three sisters helped her. They put lovely flowers in her hair. Meg was beautiful and she was very happy.

After the wedding, there was a meal at the Marches' house. Later, everybody went outside and they danced round Meg and John in the garden. Everybody enjoyed themselves very much.

At last, Meg and John went to their new home. Meg was leaving her family and she was sad about that. But she was very happy to be with her husband. She kissed her mother.

'I'll visit you every day, Marmee,' she said to her mother. 'I'm married now, but I'll always be your daughter. Thank you for my lovely, happy wedding day.'

Then Meg kissed her father and her sisters and she walked away with John. She had flowers in her hands and the June sun shone on her happy face.

That day, Meg's married life began.

2

Jo and Amy

Jo and Amy were sisters, but they were very different.

Both girls had great plans for their future lives. Amy wanted to be a painter. She had always loved to draw and she had always loved to paint.

Jo did not want to be a painter – she wanted to be a famous writer. She had started writing plays and stories many years before. Her family had always enjoyed her stories. At the age of nineteen, she still wrote a story every week. Sometimes she shut herself in her room and she wrote for hours and hours.

One day, Jo saw an advertisement in a newspaper.

'This is interesting,' she said to herself. 'There's a competition for writers. The writer of the best story will get a prize. The prize will be one hundred dollars! I'll write something for this competition.'

Jo was very excited about the competition. She did not say anything about it to her family, but she wrote a story secretly. She sent her story to the newspaper.

Six weeks passed. Jo did not hear any news about the competition. Then one day, she received a letter. She opened the envelope. Inside it was a sheet of paper and some money – banknotes for one hundred dollars! Jo read the words on the sheet of paper.

THE MASSACHUSETTS STAR

Dear Miss March,

Thank you very much for your story. It was a very good story. You have won the prize in our competition. You have won one hundred dollars. Congratulations!

Yours sincerely,
Warren R. Gree
The Editor
The Massachusetts Star

Jo was very surprised and very excited. She told her family about her story. Everybody was very happy about her prize.

'What will you do with the money, Jo?' asked Amy.

Jo thought for a moment. Then she spoke.

'I'll send Beth and Marmee for a holiday by the sea,' she said. 'Beth is very thin and pale. The sea air will be good for her.'

The next week, Beth and Mrs March had a lovely holiday by the sea. And after that, Jo sold more stories to newspapers. She used the money well. She helped her family with it. She was very happy about this.

———

Amy March was a very pretty girl. She loved fine clothes and nice things. She wanted to be a painter, but she wanted to travel too. She wanted to visit Europe. And after that, she wanted to marry a rich man.

Amy was very popular. Everybody liked her. She was sweet and kind. She listened to people's troubles. She liked to visit the family's neighbours. She always wore nice clothes for these visits.

Sometimes Jo visited the neighbours with her sister. But Jo did not enjoy these visits. She had a kind heart, but she did not like visiting people. She did not like talking about unimportant things. Everybody liked Amy, but many people did not like Jo.

'Those two March girls are very different,' people said. 'One is sunshine and the other is rain! Amy March is a pretty, interesting girl. But her sister, Jo, isn't interesting at all. She doesn't say very much and she's always bored. She's always bad-tempered.'

3

Meg's New Life

Meg Brooke was very happy with her new life. She wanted to please her husband very much. But sometimes she made mistakes.

One evening, she was talking to her husband about his work. John told her about his friends at his office.

'John,' she said. 'Please invite your friends to the house. Invite them at any time. You don't have to ask me about it first. I'll always welcome your friends to our home. They'll always have a good dinner here.'

———

The next week, John invited a friend from his office to the house. His friend's name was Mr Scott. John did not ask Meg about this first.

'Meg will be happy to see Mr Scott,' John thought.

That evening, John and Mr Scott arrived at the Brookes' house at six o'clock. Usually, the front door of the house was open. But that evening, the door was shut and locked.

John was very surprised. He went to the back of the house and he looked through the open kitchen window.

Meg was inside the kitchen and she was crying. There was fruit and sugar all over the room. Red juice covered the floor.

John spoke through the window.

'What's wrong, Meg?' he asked. 'What are you doing?'

'I'm trying to make some jam from this fruit and sugar,' replied Meg. 'But I've done it very badly. I'm hot and tired and there's fruit juice everywhere! Please help me, John.'

'Meg,' said John, 'I've brought a guest for dinner. It's Mr Scott from my office. What are we going to eat this evening?'

Suddenly, Meg was angry.

'Nothing, John!' she shouted. 'I haven't cooked any dinner. Why did you bring this man here? Why didn't you ask me about it first?'

'Meg,' said John, 'why have you —'

'Oh, go away!' shouted Meg. 'And take Mr Scott with you. I don't want him in my home!'

She ran upstairs to her room.

John and Mr Scott went into the house. They had a delicious dinner of bread and cheese that evening. They laughed and they talked for a long time.

Later, Meg was very unhappy.

'Please forgive me, John,' she said. 'I was wrong. Everything was my fault. Please invite Mr Scott here again. I'll be nice to him the next time.'

After that, Mr Scott came often to Meg and John's house. He had many happy meals there and soon he was good friends with Meg.

———

Meg and John did not have very much money. But Meg had a rich friend. Her name was Sallie Moffat. Sallie loved to go shopping. Sometimes Meg went shopping with her. Sallie bought many expensive things in the stores, but Meg only bought cheap things.

One day, Meg and Sallie saw a beautiful dress in a store in the town.

'That's a lovely dress, Meg,' said Sallie. 'Why don't you buy it?'

The dress cost twenty-five dollars. Meg had twenty-five dollars, but it was money for food and other things for the house.

'I will buy that dress,' she thought. 'John will give me some more money for food. I'll give him back the money next month.'

Meg bought the dress. But later that day, she was worried.

'What will John say?' she thought. 'I've spent all our money on a dress. Why was I so stupid?'

That evening, John Brooke came home early. Meg spoke to him.

'Please, John, don't be angry with me,' she said. 'I bought a dress today. It cost twenty-five dollars. Sallie Moffat has pretty clothes. I want to have pretty clothes too. I don't like being poor all the time.'

John was very unhappy.

'I don't earn much money, Meg,' he said quietly. 'You married a poor man. You knew that! I *try* to make you happy.'

Meg ran to her husband.

'Oh, John,' she said. 'I'm sorry. I don't want to make *you* unhappy. You're my husband and I love you. I don't care about being poor. I said terrible things to you.'

The next day, Meg took the dress back to the store. She got her money back. John did not have a coat for the winter. So Meg bought him a new coat with the money. That evening, she gave the coat to John. He was happy.

'I'll never do anything so stupid again,' Meg thought.

—

A year went by. In the summer of 1868, Meg had twin babies – her two babies were born at the same time.

One of the children was a boy and the other was a girl. The boy was called Demi, and the girl was called Daisy. Meg and John were very happy.

Meg's family were very happy too. Jo, Beth and Amy came often to Meg and John's house and they helped their sister with the babies.

'They're the most wonderful babies in the world,' said Jo.

And everybody agreed with her.

4

An Exciting Journey

One day, Amy thought of a plan. She told Jo about it.

'We must visit Aunt March today,' she said. 'Put on your best dress.'

But Jo did not want to put on nice clothes. She did not want to go out. She wanted to stay at home. She wanted to write a story.

'I'm sorry, Amy,' she said. 'I'm busy today. We'll visit Aunt March another day.'

'No,' said Amy. 'We haven't seen Aunt March for a long time. She's an old lady and she enjoys our visits. We must go today.'

One of Aunt March's friends was visiting the old lady that day. Her name was Mrs Carrol. Mrs Carrol had known Aunt March for many years.

Mrs Carrol was a very rich woman. She was planning a journey to Europe. She wanted to talk to somebody on the journey – she wanted a companion. She wanted a young lady to go to Europe with her.

'You must take my niece, Jo, with you,' said Aunt March. 'Jo is very interested in Europe.'

At that moment, Jo and Amy arrived at the house. Amy's clothes were very pretty and her smiling face was pretty too. She talked pleasantly to Aunt March and Mrs Carrol. But Jo was tired and bored. She did not say much. She was thinking about her new story. Aunt March and Mrs Carrol started to talk about France. Amy was very interested.

'Do you speak French well?' Aunt March asked her.

'Oh, yes,' replied Amy happily. 'French is a beautiful language. I want to visit France one day.'

'You're a good girl, Amy,' said Aunt March. Then she spoke to Jo.

'What about you, Jo?' she asked. 'Do you speak French?'

'No! I don't speak a word of French,' replied Jo. 'I hate French. It's a very stupid language. I don't want to go to France.'

Later, the girls went home and Aunt March talked to Mrs Carrol again.

'Jo isn't interested in France,' Aunt March said. 'I was wrong. She won't be a good companion for you. She's too bad-tempered and too rude. But Amy is a lovely girl. She's young, but she's very sweet and polite. Take Amy with you to Europe. I'll pay for her journey.'

Mrs Carrol agreed, and the next morning she wrote a letter to Mrs March.

Dear Mrs March,

I'm going to Europe next month, for a long visit. I want Amy to come with me. She will be a very good companion. And she will have a wonderful holiday.

Please let her come with me.

Yours sincerely,
Eliza Carrol

Mrs March told her daughters about this letter.

'Amy will go to Europe with Mrs Carrol in two weeks' time,' she said.

Amy was very happy and excited. She ran upstairs to her room. She started to put her clothes into cases.

Jo tried to smile. She tried to be happy for Amy. But she was not happy – she was very sad. She spoke to her mother.

'Marmee, why did Mrs Carrol choose Amy?' she asked. 'Amy is young. But nice things always happen to her. Nice things never happen to me.'

'I'm sorry, Jo,' replied her mother. 'Please try to be happy for Amy.'

'It's my own fault,' said Jo sadly. 'Why was I rude and bad-tempered? I want to visit Europe very much.'

Beth had come into the room. She had heard her sister's words. She ran across the room and she put her arms round Jo.

'Please don't go away to Europe, dear Jo,' she said. 'Please stay at home with me.'

Jo smiled at Beth and soon she was happy again.

———

For the next few weeks, everybody was very busy. Amy needed a lot of things for her visit – clothes, books, paints and brushes.

'I'm going to paint a lot of pictures on this holiday,' she told her family.

At last, it was the day of the journey. The March family travelled to New York with Mrs Carrol and Amy. Laurie went with them too.

The next afternoon, Amy was standing on the deck of a great ship in New York harbour.

Far below her, Amy saw her family and Laurie. They were waving goodbye.

Suddenly, Amy was sad and lonely.

'I'm going very far away,' she thought. 'And I love my family very much. When will I see them again?'

Slowly, the great ship left the harbour. The bright summer sun shone on the ocean. The March family watched the ship for a long time. At last, they could no longer see it.

Amy sent letters to her family from London, then from Paris.

London

Dear Everybody,

I'm having a wonderful time in London. We often drive through the city in a carriage.
It has rained a lot, but today the weather was better. We had a lovely picnic in Richmond Park.
There are many fine old buildings in London. There are many nice stores too. Some of the best stores are in Regent Street. Clothes are cheaper here than in America. Mrs Carrol bought me two new dresses and some hats.

All my love to you,

Amy

Paris

Dear Everybody,

Now we are staying in Paris. There are so many interesting things in this beautiful city. I often visit the Louvre - the famous art museum. The pictures there are wonderful. I also like walking in the Tuileries Gardens. They are lovely. There are so many interesting people in Paris. Mrs Carrol and I like sitting in the cafés. We watch people walking past us in the streets.

All my love to you,

Amy

5

Trouble for Jo

One day in early October, Mrs March spoke seriously to Jo about her sister Beth.

'I'm not happy about her,' said Mrs March. 'Beth is so sad and quiet. Is she worried about something?'

'I don't know, Marmee,' replied Jo.

'And what about you, Jo?' her mother said. 'You're very quiet too. Are *you* worried about anything? Can I help you?'

'Well,' said Jo. 'I want to ask you about something. I have a plan. I want to go away this winter. I want to go to New York.'

'You want to go to New York?' Mrs March said. She was surprised. 'Tell me, Jo – why do you want to go away?'

At first Jo did not reply. But after a few moments, she spoke quietly.

'Well, Marmee – I want to get away from Laurie,' she said. 'Laurie has written lots of letters to me this summer. And he wants to speak to me about something important. He told me that in his last letter.'

'Dear Jo – Laurie loves you,' her mother said. 'Do you love him?'

'I like him very much – he's my dearest friend,' Jo replied. 'But I don't want to marry him, Marmee. I don't want to be his wife.'

'I understand,' said Mrs March kindly. 'And you're right, Jo. You must go away for a few months. A friend of mine lives in New York. Her name is Mrs Kirke. I've known her for many years. You must stay with her. I'll write to her tonight.'

———

A few days later, Mrs March had a letter from Mrs Kirke.

Dear Mary,

Thank you for your nice letter. I'll be very happy to have Jo in my house. I want to meet her very much. She is a clever girl – you have told me that. Can she teach? Will she teach my two little girls for a few hours every day?

    My best wishes to you,

    Louisa Kirke

The next day, Laurie left his college for the last time. He came home to his grandfather's house. The day after that, he visited Jo.

'Please come for a walk with me, Jo,' the young man said.

Jo and Laurie walked in the woods near the town. At first, they were both silent. Then Jo spoke.

'Laurie, you've finished your studies now,' she said. 'What are you going to do next?'

'I'm going to have a long holiday,' replied Laurie. 'And then —'

He stopped and he looked down at Jo's face.

'Jo, I want to tell you something,' he said.

Jo put her hand on Laurie's arm.

'No, Laurie,' she said. 'Please don't tell me.'

'But I must tell you,' replied Laurie. 'I'm in love with you, Jo. I've always loved you. And now I want to marry you.'

Jo was silent for a few seconds. Laurie waited.

'Dear Laurie,' she said at last. Her voice was sad. 'I'll always be your special friend. But I don't want to marry you. Please don't be unhappy. One day, you'll meet a lovely girl. You'll fall in love with her and you'll marry her. You'll forget about me.'

Laurie's face became pale. He was very unhappy.

'No, Jo,' he said. 'You don't understand. I'll never love anybody else. And I'll never forget you – never, never!'

Then he walked quickly away through the woods.

'Oh!' thought Jo. 'What shall I do now?'

She went quickly to Laurie's house. She wanted to talk to Laurie's grandfather. Mr Laurence was at home, and Jo told him about Laurie's unhappiness. The old man listened carefully.

'I'm worried about Laurie, sir,' Jo said. 'Please be kind to him.'

'You're a fine girl, Jo,' said Mr Laurence. 'And you're right. You don't love my grandson and you mustn't marry him. I understand. I'll talk to Laurie.'

'Thank you, sir,' replied Jo.

That evening, Laurie was very sad and quiet. And old Mr Laurence was very sad for his grandson.

'Laurie, I know about you and Jo,' he said. 'Jo told me everything. You can't do anything about this. Jo isn't going to change her mind.'

Laurie did not reply.

31

'Listen to me! I have a good plan,' the old man said. 'We'll visit Europe together. We'll go to interesting places and we'll see wonderful things. What do you say, Laurie?'

At first, Laurie was not interested in his grandfather's plan. But at last, he agreed. Mr Laurence was very pleased.

———

A week later, Laurie and Mr Laurence left the little town. They travelled to New York. Then they got on a ship and they started their journey to Europe.

A few days after that, Jo went to New York too. A new part of her life was beginning.

'Soon, the winter will come,' she thought. 'Will the winter bring me happiness?'

6

A New Friend

Jo was very happy in New York. She often thought about her family, but she enjoyed her new life. Everything in the city was very interesting. Every week, she wrote a letter to her family. In the first letter, she told them about Mrs Kirke's home.

New York   November

Dear Marmee, Father and Beth,
    Here I am in New York. Mrs Kirke has welcomed me into her house. She is a very kind lady.
    My room is at the top of the house. I have to climb many stairs, but the view of the city from my room is wonderful! I have a small table for writing.
    Every day, I teach Mrs Kirke's little girls. But in the evening I have free time.

Sometimes, I stay in my room and I write stories. Sometimes, I go downstairs and I talk to the other people in the house. There are several other people living here. They pay Mrs Kirke for a room in her house. These people work in New York, but they come from other places.

I'll write again soon.

Lots of love from,

Jo

The next week, Jo wrote again.

New York

Dear Marmee, Father and Beth,
   I've had a busy week, but I'm enjoying myself very much. Teaching is hard work. Mrs Kirke's little girls are sweet, but sometimes they're very naughty.
   I've met an interesting man here. His name is Professor Bhaer.

The Professor is staying in Mrs Kirke's boarding-house too. He comes from Berlin, in Germany. He's working in New York - he teaches German to people.

Professor Bhaer isn't a young man, he's about forty. He isn't good-looking, but he has a nice face and kind brown eyes. He doesn't have much money and he doesn't have fine clothes. But he loves books and music, and he knows many interesting things. I enjoy talking to him very much. He's going to teach me German.

That's all my news for now. Lots of love from,
Jo

During the next few weeks, Jo and Professor Bhaer became good friends. The Professor was a good man. Jo liked being with him very much. They both liked books, paintings and music and they often talked about these things.

The Professor was a kind man and he was a very clever man too. He often helped Jo, and he gave her good advice. She always listened to his advice.

Jo was very busy with Mrs Kirke's children, but she wrote stories in the evenings. The Professor was very interested in Jo's stories. At Christmas, he gave her a book of Shakespeare's plays.

'You're going to be a writer,' he said. 'You must learn about people. You will learn a lot about people from these plays.'

Everybody had a wonderful time in Mrs Kirke's house at Christmas. Jo's family sent a big parcel of food and letters to her. Mrs Kirke cooked a lovely dinner.

After dinner, all the people in the house put on brightly-coloured clothes and they acted in a play. It was very good fun.

Then Jo remembered Christmases at home with her sisters, and she was happy. She told the Professor about Christmases at the Marches' house.

'Every year, I wrote a play,' she said. 'My sisters and I acted in the play for our friends.'

———

Jo was not rich. She wanted to earn some money. One day, she wrote a story and she sold it to a newspaper. The paper was called *The Weekly Volcano*. The editor paid her a lot of money for her story. But the *Volcano* was not a good newspaper. Jo's story was a good story, but the editor of the paper changed it. After that, the story was not her own work any more.

During the next weeks, Jo wrote a lot of stories for the *Volcano*. The editor printed stories about murders and stories about ghosts. Jo wrote stories about these things. But she was not proud of them. She did not tell anybody about them.

One day, the Professor saw Jo reading *The Weekly Volcano*. He was very surprised.

'Why are you reading the *Volcano*, Jo?' he asked. 'It's a terrible paper. There are lots of stories in it – that's true. But they aren't good stories. Your stories are very good, Jo. One day, you'll write a great book.'

'I want to write a great book, Professor,' Jo said.

'You will write one, Jo,' the Professor replied. 'Please don't read the *Volcano* any more. You won't learn anything from it.'

Jo thought about the Professor's words.

'Professor Bhaer is right,' she said to herself. '*The Weekly Volcano* is a terrible paper. It pays me well, but it isn't a good paper for my stories. I mustn't write for it any more. I don't know about murderers and ghosts. I know about ordinary people.'

After that, Jo wrote a different kind of story. She wrote stories about ordinary people. She did not earn much money, but she was happy.

———

Jo stayed at Mrs Kirke's house for six months. The time passed very quickly. Soon it was June 1869. One morning, Jo spoke to Professor Bhaer.

'I'm going to return to my home tomorrow,' she said. 'Please come to our town one day. I want you to meet my family.'

'Thank you, Jo,' replied the Professor. 'I'll be very happy to meet your family.'

'And I want you to meet Laurie too,' Jo said.

'Who is Laurie?' asked the Professor.

'Laurie is my best friend,' replied Jo.

'Oh,' said the Professor. Suddenly, he was very sad. But Jo did not see the sadness in her friend's face.

'Jo is in love with this young man,' the Professor thought. 'She likes me, but I'm only her friend. And I'm twenty years older than her. There's no place for me in Jo's life.'

The next morning, Jo started on her journey. The Professor went with her to the train station.

'Goodbye, dear Jo,' he said. 'Be happy!'

Jo got into a train. Soon it was moving out of the
station.

'The winter has gone,' she thought.

7

A New Beginning

In November 1868, Laurie and his grandfather were in France. At first, they stayed in Paris. Old Mr Laurence liked Paris, but Laurie was not happy there. He thought about Jo all the time. His grandfather was worried about him.

'Amy March is in Nice, in the south of France,' said Mr Laurence. 'She is there with Mrs Carrol. It will be Christmas soon. Why don't you go and visit Amy for Christmas?'

'All right, Grandfather,' said Laurie. 'I'll go to Nice for a week in December.'

———

Laurie arrived in Nice on the afternoon before Christmas Day. Amy was walking by the sea that afternoon. Suddenly, she saw a tall young man walking towards her. He was smiling at her.

'Who *is* that young man?' she thought. 'I've seen him before, but where have I seen him?'

'Good afternoon, Amy,' said the young man.

'Laurie!' said Amy. She was very happy to see him. 'You've changed – you've changed so much.'

This was true. Laurie was no longer a boy. He was a tall, handsome young man. In the streets, many young ladies looked at him and they smiled at him.

That evening, there was a Christmas party in Amy's

hotel. Amy invited Laurie to the party.

Amy wore a lovely white dress and she had flowers in her hair. She was beautiful. Many young men wanted to dance with her.

'Amy was right,' thought Laurie. 'I have changed. But she has changed too. She's not a child any more. She's a beautiful woman.'

Amy was thinking about Laurie.

'There's something wrong with Laurie,' she said to herself. 'His face is so sad. Why is he so unhappy?'

———

Laurie did not return to Paris after Christmas. He stayed in Nice for a month. He and Amy met each other every day. Amy always wanted to go out. She wanted to visit interesting places. But Laurie never wanted to go anywhere. Amy was very surprised about this. She could not understand it.

One afternoon, Amy thought of a plan.

'It's a lovely day today,' she said to Laurie. 'Let's go to Valrosa. It's a beautiful place by the sea. I will paint a picture there.'

'No, Amy. It's too warm,' replied Laurie. 'Let's stay inside the hotel.'

'No,' said Amy. 'I want to go out. Please come with me, Laurie.'

'All right,' Laurie said at last. 'But I'm tired. It's a long way to Valrosa. I don't want to drive a carriage there, Amy. It will be hard work.'

'I'll drive the carriage,' Amy replied.

Amy drove the small carriage to Valrosa. The views of the coast and the sea were very beautiful. The sea was blue and the sun was shining. It was early spring, and there were flowers everywhere.

At Valrosa, Laurie lay on the grass. Amy painted a picture of him.

For a long time, Amy did not speak. But she was thinking hard.

'I must tell the truth to Laurie,' she thought. 'He's my friend. I don't want to say bad things about him. I don't want to hurt him. But I want to understand his unhappiness.'

Amy spoke seriously to her friend.

'You've changed a lot, Laurie,' she said. 'You've become very lazy. You don't care about anything now. You're wasting your life. What's wrong with you? What will Jo say about you?'

At first, Laurie did not reply. Then, after a minute, he spoke quietly and sadly.

'Jo won't say anything about me,' he said. 'She doesn't care about me.'

'Oh!' thought Amy. 'Laurie was Jo's special friend, but he doesn't talk about her any more. And now he says, "She doesn't care about me." That's very strange. Has something bad happened between them? I must find out more about this.'

Amy spoke gently to Laurie.

'Is Jo angry with you?' she asked.

'Please don't ask me about Jo,' replied Laurie. 'I love Jo. I love her very much, but she doesn't love me.'

'Now I understand,' said Amy. 'Jo doesn't love you. And now you don't care about anything any more. You don't care about other people. But you mustn't waste your life, Laurie. You are a man now, and you must do something useful.'

Laurie said nothing.

'Think about your grandfather, Laurie,' Amy said. 'He loves you and he's waiting for you in Paris. Why don't you go and see him?'

Laurie did not like Amy's words. But he listened to them and he thought about them.

'Amy is right,' he thought. 'I must do something. I mustn't waste my life.'

The next day, Amy received a note from Laurie.

> Dear Amy,
>
> I have gone back to Paris.
>
> Best wishes,
>
> Lazy Laurie

'Oh!' thought Amy. 'Laurie is angry with *me* now. He doesn't want to stay here with me!'

———

Laurie stayed in Paris for a few weeks, then, in March, he went to Vienna. There, he was happier. He met a lot of people and he visited many interesting places. But he could not forget Amy's words.

'Amy will change her mind about me,' he thought. 'I'm not lazy and I *can* do something useful with my life.'

The weeks passed. Sometimes Laurie thought about Jo, but he was no longer unhappy about her. And every day he thought about Amy. 'What is she doing today?' he often asked himself. He wanted to see her again very much. So at last, he went back to Nice.

———

It was a sunny afternoon in late April. Amy was sitting alone in a garden near the sea. She was reading a letter from home and she was thinking about her mother and her father and her sisters. Her pretty face was sad. But suddenly, she looked up and she saw Laurie coming towards her.

'Oh, Laurie!' she said. 'This is a lovely surprise! I'm so happy to see you. But I've had some bad news from home. Mother is worried about Beth. I must go back to America soon.'

Laurie was sad about Amy's news. But he was very happy to be with her again. They walked in the garden and they talked for a long time. And that day, they began to fall in love.

A few days later, Amy and Laurie were sitting in a boat on a lake near Amy's hotel. Everything was very beautiful and peaceful.

'I love you, Amy,' said Laurie quietly. 'I love you very much. Will you marry me?'

'Yes, dear Laurie,' replied Amy. 'One day, I will marry you.'

8

A Sad Time

It was July 1869. Amy was still in France, but Jo had returned home from New York. She was very happy to be with her family again. But she was worried about her favourite sister, Beth. Beth had changed. She was very quiet. Often, she sat alone in her room and she cried.

'Beth must have another holiday,' Jo thought. 'I must take her to the sea.'

———

Jo and Beth stayed in a little house by the sea for a month. The sisters had a lovely time. The days passed quietly. They talked a lot and they went for short walks.

One afternoon, they were sitting peacefully by the sea. The sun was shining. Beth put her hand on Jo's arm and she spoke quietly to her sister.

'Jo, dear,' she said. 'I want to tell you something. I'm going to die soon.'

Suddenly, Jo was very sad and very frightened.

'No, Beth, no!' she said. 'You're wrong. You're only nineteen. You mustn't die. You mustn't leave me.'

'Please don't be sad, Jo,' said Beth. 'I'm ill and I'm not going to get better. But I am happy.'

At that moment, a white bird flew over their heads. The two girls watched it. It was beautiful. Then Beth saw a little brown bird walking on the sand. This little bird was not beautiful, but it was sweet and friendly.

'You're the white bird, Jo,' said Beth. 'You're strong and beautiful and you're not afraid of anything. But I'm the little brown bird. I haven't done many things in my life, but I've been happy. Meg and Amy always wanted fine clothes. I never wanted fine clothes. You wanted an exciting life, Jo. I never wanted that. You all wanted to leave home. You all wanted to have adventures. But I only wanted to stay at home with Marmee and Father.'

Jo's eyes were full of tears.

'What shall I do for you, Beth?' she asked quietly. 'Tell me, my dearest sister.'

'Please Jo, will you tell Marmee and Father my news?' Beth said. 'Marmee is worried about me, but she doesn't know about my illness.'

A few days later, Jo and Beth went home. Beth was tired after the journey and she went to bed early.

'How am I going to tell Marmee and Father about Beth?' Jo asked herself.

But at that moment, Mrs March came to Jo. She looked at her daughter's sad face, and she put her arms round the unhappy girl.

'You don't have to tell me your news, Jo,' she said. 'I know about Beth. She's going to die. We must all be strong for her, Jo. She won't live for very long now. We must make her last months very happy.'

The next day, Mr March moved Beth's bed into the prettiest room in the house. Mrs March and Jo put beautiful flowers, books and pictures in the room. Beth's piano was there too. She still loved to play it.

Beth's room was a happy place. It was warm and sunny. Lots of visitors came to see her there. Beth was interested in everybody's news. Meg often brought her twin babies, Demi and Daisy. Amy sent letters and cards to her from Europe. Amy was happy in Europe and Beth did not want her to come home.

The summer passed. Autumn and winter passed. In the spring, Beth began to get very tired. She stayed in bed for most of each day. She could not read or talk much. She did not play her piano any more.

Jo slept in Beth's room every night. She took care of Beth and she did everything for her sister. She fed her and she read stories to her. Jo was very happy to look after Beth. But sometimes Beth's pain was terrible and Jo couldn't help her. On those days, Jo was very sad and worried.

'My dear Jo,' said Beth one morning. 'Make me a promise. Marmee and Father will be very unhappy after my death. Please help them. Please take care of them.'

'I'll try to do that, Beth,' said Jo sadly.

'Beth is so brave and good,' Jo thought. 'She always thinks about other people. She never thinks about herself.'

The days became longer and warmer. That spring was very beautiful. The trees were green again and there were flowers everywhere in the garden.

Beth died early one morning. Her mother and her father were with her. Meg and Jo were with her too. Beth's face was very peaceful. Her pain had gone.

'Beth is happy again now,' said Mrs March.

Beth's body lay on the bed. Outside in the garden, a bird began to sing. The light of the sun came through the window and it touched the dead girl's cold face.

Jo sat near Beth's bed and she cried for hours and hours. At last, she stood up and walked towards the door.

'I'll never forget you, my dear little sister,' she said.

9

'You're a Married Man Now'

Jo's life was difficult after her sister's death. She had taken care of Beth for nearly a year. She was very sad and lonely without her. Jo was not interested in anything any more. She thought about her dead sister all the time.

'My life is empty and useless now,' she thought.

Sometimes she could not sleep at night. She lay awake in her bed and she thought about her sister.

'Oh, Beth! Come back!' she said to herself.

She often talked to her mother and father about Beth. She also talked to Meg. Meg often thought about Beth too. But she was very busy with her own life. She had her husband, John, and her children, Demi and Daisy.

'Meg is happy with her life,' thought Jo. 'I want to be happy too. Will I get married one day? Will anybody marry me?'

The days passed slowly. Jo lived quietly at home with her parents. She helped her mother with the housework and she started writing stories again. But she often remembered her happy months in New York. She often thought about her friends in the city.

'I don't want to stay at home all my life,' she thought.

One day, the family received a letter from Amy.

Nice   May 1870

Dear Everybody,

I have some wonderful news.
Laurie and I are engaged.
We will come back to America
very soon.

All my love to you,
Amy

Mr and Mrs March were very happy. But Mrs March spoke to Jo alone.

'Jo, what do you think about Amy and Laurie's engagement?' she asked. 'Laurie was your special friend. Now he's going to marry Amy. Are you happy about that?'

'Oh, yes, Marmee,' replied Jo. 'It's wonderful news. I'm very happy for Amy and Laurie.'

But Mrs March was worried about Jo.

'Dear Jo,' she thought. 'She took care of Beth so well. And now she's very lonely. Meg has John and her children, and now Amy has Laurie. But Jo has nobody.'

The weeks passed. One evening, Jo was standing by the kitchen window. She was thinking about New York and about her friends there.

Suddenly she looked up and she saw Laurie's face outside the window. He was smiling at her. His face was very happy.

'Laurie!' said Jo. 'This is a wonderful surprise!'

She opened the front door and Laurie came into the house.

'I'm very happy to see you,' Jo said. 'But where is Amy?'

'My wife is at Meg's house with your mother,' replied Laurie.

'Your *wife*!' said Jo. 'Are you and Amy married? Why didn't you write to us about your wedding?'

'We wanted to surprise you,' said Laurie. 'We heard the news about Beth's death and we were very sad. We got married in Paris, but we had a very quiet wedding. Then we started on our return journey.'

'Well, Laurie,' said Jo. 'You're a married man now. Tell me all your other news.'

Jo and Laurie talked for a long time. Laurie laughed a lot and he told Jo funny stories about his journeys in Europe. Then suddenly, he was very serious.

'I want to tell you something, Jo,' he said. 'I was very unhappy eighteen months ago. But you were right about us. I understand that now. And now, Amy and I love each other very much. But you and I will always be good friends.'

'Dear Laurie,' said Jo. 'You are my brother now. And I'll always love my brother.'

At that moment, the whole family came into the room. Old Mr Laurence and John Brooke were with them. Everybody was very happy and excited. Amy was wearing a fine dress from Paris. Her eyes were bright and she was very beautiful. Laurie looked at his wife. There was love in his eyes. Jo saw this and she was very happy.

Later, Jo was alone in the kitchen. All the others were upstairs. They were talking and they were singing. Suddenly, Jo was very lonely again.

'I'm very happy about Laurie and Amy,' she thought. 'Why am I so sad about myself?'

10

A Welcome Visitor

At that moment, somebody knocked loudly at the front door. Jo opened the door and she saw a man standing outside. He turned around and looked at her. It was Professor Bhaer!

'Oh, Professor Bhaer! I'm so happy to see you!' said Jo. She put her hand on her friend's arm and she led him into the house.

'And I'm very happy to see you again, Jo,' replied the Professor. Then he heard people talking and laughing upstairs.

'Are you having a party?' he asked.

'No,' Jo replied. 'My sister Amy and her husband have come home from Europe. All my family are here. You must meet them.'

Jo closed the door and she led the Professor upstairs.

'Marmee, Father – this is Professor Bhaer, my friend from New York,' she said.

Everybody was happy to see the Professor. Mr March welcomed him to the house. The Professor talked to Jo's parents and to Meg and John for a few minutes. Then Jo led the Professor towards Laurie.

'Professor Bhaer, this is my dear, special friend Laurie Laurence,' she said.

'Oh,' thought the Professor sadly. 'This is Jo's young man. He's very good-looking.'

Then Jo called to her younger sister.

'And this is my sister, Amy,' Jo said to Professor Bhaer. 'She is Laurie's wife.'

Suddenly the Professor was happy again. The handsome young man was not married to Jo, he was married to her sister!

Professor Bhaer enjoyed a wonderful evening with Jo and her family. Everybody liked him. Everybody talked to him. Meg's children played with him.

At last, the Professor had to leave.

'Please come here again soon, Professor,' said Mrs March. 'We'll always welcome you to our home.'

'Thank you, I will come again soon,' replied the Professor. 'I'll be in your town for a few weeks. I have some business here.'

———

After that, the Professor visited the Marches' house often. Jo was always happy to see him. Her mother and father watched her talking to the Professor.

'Jo is very happy with Professor Bhaer,' Mrs March said to her husband. 'That's good. She doesn't have many friends. The Professor is a very nice man. And he's very clever too.'

For two weeks, Professor Bhaer visited the house every day. Then he did not come for three days. At first, Jo was sad. After that, she became angry.

'I don't understand this,' she thought. 'Where is the Professor? Has he gone away? Why didn't he say goodbye to me?'

Then she thought of a plan.

'The Professor is staying in the town,' she thought. 'I'll go out now. I'll look for him.'

Jo spoke to her mother. 'I'm going to walk to the stores,' she said. 'I'm going to do some shopping.'

'It's going to rain,' Mrs March replied. 'Take your umbrella with you, Jo.'

Jo put on a pretty new hat and her best coat. But she forgot about her umbrella. She walked into the town. She went into three or four stores but she did not see the Professor.

Then it began to rain. Jo ran across the street

towards some more stores.

Suddenly, somebody held a big umbrella over her head.

'Hello, Jo,' Professor Bhaer said. 'What are you doing here?'

Jo's hat and hair and clothes were very wet.

'I'm doing some shopping,' she replied.

'I have to do some shopping too,' said the Professor. 'Please help me with my shopping. I'll hold the umbrella for you.'

The Professor and Jo went into a store.

———

An hour later, Professor Bhaer and Jo had finished their shopping.

'Will you come to our house now?' Jo asked. 'Will you drink some tea with us?'

They walked back to the Marches' house together.

'I have some news, Jo,' Professor Bhaer said. 'My business here is finished. I'm not going to return to New York. A friend of mine owns a school here in America. I'm going to be a teacher at the school. I must earn some more money.'

'That's wonderful news,' said Jo. 'We'll meet each other often.'

'No,' said the Professor. 'We will not meet often. The school is very far away. It's in the state of Iowa.'

'Oh,' said Jo and her eyes filled with tears.

'The Professor is going to leave me,' she thought. 'He doesn't care about me.'

The Professor looked at his friend's sad face.

'Jo, my dear love,' he said quietly. 'Why are you crying?'

'You're going to leave me,' said Jo. 'I'll never see you again!'

'Jo, listen to me,' the Professor said. 'I love you. Do you love me too? I want to marry you, but I'm a poor man.'

'I don't care about that,' said Jo. 'I don't want a rich husband. I want you. I love you more than anything in the world.'

They came to the Marches' house. They stood outside the front door.

Professor Bhaer spoke again.

'I can only give you my heart and my empty hands,' he said.

Jo looked up at him. There was love in her eyes. She put her hands into the Professor's hands.

'Your hands aren't empty now, my dear,' she said.

Then she led the Professor into the house and she closed the door.

11

Happy Families

Professor Bhaer went to Iowa. He taught at his friend's school. The Professor wanted to earn some money before his marriage to Jo. He wrote to her every week and she wrote to him.

In 1872, Aunt March suddenly became ill and she died a few days later. After that, her big old house – Plumfield – belonged to Jo.

'Will you sell Plumfield?' Laurie asked Jo one day. 'It's a fine old house and you'll get a lot of money for it.'

'No, I'm not going to sell Plumfield,' replied Jo. 'The Professor and I are going to get married soon. We will live there.'

'But Jo, the house and the garden are so big,' said Laurie. 'Why do you want to live there?'

'We're going to have a school for boys,' Jo replied. 'I've had this plan for a long time, but I couldn't buy a house. I didn't have any money.'

'Now I own a house!' said Jo. 'There will be rich boys at the school, but there will be poor boys too. The Professor will teach them. I will cook for them and take care of them.'

At first Jo's family were surprised. But they were happy about her plan.

'It's a wonderful plan, Jo,' said Mrs March.

'There will be a lot of hard work for me,' said Jo.

'Yes. But you will do it – I know that,' said her mother. 'And we'll all help you.'

———

That summer, Professor Bhaer left his job in Iowa and he and Jo got married. They lived at Plumfield and they had their school there.

Mrs March was right – the work was hard! But Jo did not care about that. She and the Professor were not rich, but they were very happy. They loved their school and they were very kind to the boys. Sometimes the boys were naughty. But Jo and the Professor helped them and took good care of them. Plumfield was soon a very fine school.

After a few years, Jo and her husband had two children of their own. They were both boys – Rob and Teddy.

Amy and Laurie had a child too – a girl. They called her Beth.

Every year, in October, there was a special holiday at Jo's school. This was the apple-picking holiday. There were many apple trees in the large garden at Plumfield. During the October holiday, Jo and the Professor and their boys picked the apples. All the families helped them – Mr and Mrs March, Meg and her husband and their children, and Amy and Laurie and their daughter.

———

It was October 1877 – five years after Jo's wedding. It was the apple-picking holiday. It was also Mrs March's birthday. She was sixty years old.

Everybody worked hard that day. They picked all the apples. Then they had a wonderful picnic on the

grass, under the trees. The golden sun shone from a clear blue sky.

Mrs March had many lovely birthday presents.

'You've done so many things for us, dear Marmee,' Meg said to her mother.

'Yes, you've helped us all so much,' said Jo.

'Thank you for everything,' said Amy.

'Yes, thank you for everything,' Meg and Jo said.

Soon, it was the end of a wonderful day. All the children ran around the garden. They climbed the trees and they played happily together. Jo watched her husband and her two boys. She was very happy. She put her arms round Meg and Amy, her dear sisters.

'Families are the most beautiful things in the world,' she said.

Published by Macmillan Heinemann ELT
Between Towns Road, Oxford OX4 3PP
Macmillan Heinemann ELT is an imprint of
Macmillan Publishers Limited
Companies and representatives throughout the world
Heinemann is a registered trademark of Harcourt Education, used under licence.

ISBN 1–405072–30–X
EAN 978–1–405072–30–4

This retold version by Anne Collins for Macmillan Readers
First published 1999
Text © Anne Collins 1999, 2005
Design and illustration © Macmillan Publishers Limited 1999, 2005

This edition first published 2005

Designed by Sue Vaudin
Illustrated by Barry Wilkinson
Map on page 3 by Peter Harper
Typography by Adrian Hodgkins
Original cover template design by Jackie Hill
Cover illustration by Getty/Bridgeman Art Library
Acknowledgements: The publishers would like to thank Popperfoto for
permission to reproduce the picture on page 4.

Printed in Thailand

2009 2008 2007 2006 2005
10 9 8 7 6 5 4 3 2 1